The Basic Essentials of
SEA KAYAKING

by Mike Wyatt

Illustrations by
Denise Harris

ICS BOOKS, Inc.
Merrillville, Indiana

THE BASIC ESSENTIALS OF SEA KAYAKING

10 9 8 7 6 5 4 3 2 1

Printed in U.S.A.

ACKNOWLEDGMENTS

To Tim Davis of Pacific Water Sports for his support and criticism, and to John Meyer of the Northwest Outdoor Center for his kind assistance in preparing the illustrations.

Published by:
ICS BOOKS, Inc
1370 E. 86th Place
Merrillville, IN 46410
800-541-7323

Library of Congress Cataloging-in-Publication Data

Wyatt, Mike, 1953-
   Sea kayaking : the basic essentials of / by Mike Wyatt :
illustrated by Denise Harris.
      p.   cm. -- (The Basic essentials series)
    ISBN 0-934802-55-6 : $4.95
     1. Sea kayaking. I. Harris, Denise. II. Title. III. Title:
Basic essentials of sea kayaking.
GV788.5.W93 1990
797.1'22--dc20

90-33354
CIP

TABLE OF CONTENTS

1. THE BOAT

What is a Sea Kayak?

A kayak is a closed-deck boat with an open area near the middle where the paddler sits. Propulsion and steering are provided by a two-bladed paddle. If a kayak carries one person, it's called a K-1 or a single. If it carries two people, it's known variously as a K-2, tandem or double. Kayaks can be roughly divided into three categories: sea kayaks, white,water kayaks and flat,water kayaks.

Sea kayaks differ as greatly from their whitewater and flat,water counterparts as an ocean differs from a river or a lake. Each category is shaped by the widely differing environments for which they're intended. Within each category are further divisions of distinct types of kayaks uniquely adapted for regional conditions and paddling styles. The major divisions of sea kayaks are: surf skis, wave skis, open cockpit touring, sport touring and general touring.

Types of Sea Kayaks

Surf Skis: Surf skis began as ocean rescue craft in Australia and South Africa. Introduced to the U.S. in the late '70s, these sleek, fast and sexy boats have come into their own in warm waters and surf of Hawaii, Southern California and the southeast where they are popular for racing, fitness paddling and surfing.

Racing surf skis average 19 feet long with a narrow beam of only 17 inches—clearly built for speed, not stability. Recreational models top out with a beam of 20 inches, still narrow by conventional ocean kayak standards. Surf skis weigh an average of 35 pounds and are made using the same materials and techniques as fiberglass, ocean touring kayaks. Most surf skis lack storage compartments and have a foot-pedal controlled rudder, resembling a surfboard skeg, placed along the centerline of the hull a few feet forward of the stern. When used for surfing, the bow is fitted with a "snitch," a winged extension that keeps the boat from nosing into the water when traveling down the face of a wave.

Wave Skis: Wave skis are the squat cousins of surfskis they look like a cross between a kayak and a surfboard. They average seven to nine feet in length with a two-foot beam. They have flat, planing hulls and are very stable, though sluggish at typical touring speeds when compared to the displacement hull of more conventional ocean kayaks. Wave skis are built of fiberglass and resin applied over a solid foam core. Like surf skis, they have a seat and footwells molded into a watertight deck, making exit and entry on the water much easier.

Wave skis can be divided into two types. The majority are performance play boats built for the surf. They have no interior storage and are not well-suited to touring. Recreational models feature longer designs and interior storage. They're suitable for warm water day tripping and overnight touring when great quantities of gear will not be carried.

Open Cockpit Touring Kayaks: These hybrid boats combine features found in surf skis and wave skis with those found in conventional sea touring kayaks: A self-bailing open cockpit set into a deck with hatch-accessed stowage atop a beamy displacement hull. They range in length from 13 to 16 feet. The best known example of these boats is the Scupper, a rotomolded polyethylene kayak with a 14 foot length and 26 inch beam. A number of makes and models of open cockpit

Figure 1   Types of Sea Kayaks

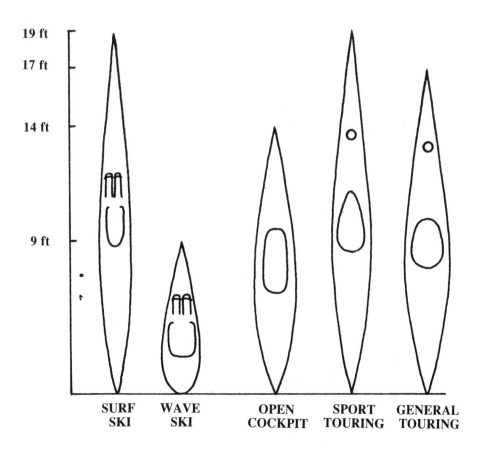

touring kayaks are available in polyethylene or fiberglass/resin construction. Some models include SCUBA tank storage compartments for divers. These boats are best suited to warm water environments.

Sport Touring Kayaks: These long, narrow and quick boats are the responsive sports cars of touring kayaks. Like a sports car, they require a higher level of attentiveness and skill to operate, their cockpit can be a bit cramped, and they aren't the best choice for loading up with camping gear and heading out on a long trip, but they are exciting to travel in. At 17 to 19 feet long with a 20 to 22 inch beam, these boats are less stable than general touring kayaks and are best suited to skills-intensive paddlers not looking for a stable, easy-paddling platform.

General Touring Kayaks: Designed to be stable, comfortable and easy to paddle at cruising speeds, general touring kayaks are built to carry the loads necessary to support a paddler on a long trip. These boats average 15 to 18 feet in length with a beam of from 23 to 26 inches. Their wider beam means a boat somewhat slower than a sport touring kayak, but the added stability is suited to a wider range of skill levels and allows for a greater number of uses, including photography, bird watching and fishing. The majority of recreational sea kayaks, including boats made of fiberglass, polyethylene and fabric/frame construction are of this type. General touring kayaks are the focus of this book.

Materials & Construction

Fiberglass: The majority of sea kayaks are made of a molded fiberglass and resin composite. This combination of materials produces a lightweight, strong and durable boat for a reasonable price. General touring sea kayaks typically weigh between 50 to 60 lbs for a single and 80 to 90 lbs for a double.

Polyester is the most commonly used resin, followed by the more expensive vinylester resin, which is preferred by some of the best manufacturers for its greater flexibility. Epoxy, the toughest of the three plastics, is also used, but difficulty with repairs and its higher toxicity during the molding process limit its popularity.

Three types of fiberglass material are commonly used in various combinations to reinforce critical areas of the hull and deck: cloth, with the finest weave, highest tensile strength, and least absorbtion; woven roving, with a broader, more coarse weave; and mat, random strands of fiberglass matted together, with highest absorbency and stiffness.

Fiberglass kayaks are molded in two parts, the hull and deck, which are then joined. The molding process begins with the spray application of the gel-coat, a tough layer of abrasion resistant resin that will eventually form the outer skin of the boat. Usually an opaque color, the gel-coat helps protect the underlying materials from the damaging effects of the sun's ultraviolet radiation and gives the finished boat a cosmetically pleasing, evenly-colored surface.

The next steps employ one of two construction methods: hand lay-up or vacuum bagging. In a hand lay-up, all of the materials are manipulated by hand. Vacuum bagging is exactly what it sounds like: After the gel-coat has been applied to the mold surface, fiberglass material and the resin are placed in the mold, a plastic sheet is placed on top and sealed around the edges of the mold. A vacuum pump is applied and the air is removed, compressing and saturating the fiberglass material with resin and forcing any air bubbles and excess resin from between the mold and the plastic bag.

There is no intrinsic advantage in either method of construction. Hand lay-up allows greater control of the materials, but also requires greater skill to execute successfully. A skilled craftsperson can produce a superior boat using this method of construction, but a less skilled builder will produce spotty results. Vacuum bagging is attractive to manufacturers because it will generally produce more consistent results with less skilled builders. Its major drawback is the difficulty in controlling the amount of resin present in the lamination. The decks and hulls of boats built by this method are frequently thinner than is desirable. Some manufacturers are working with a thicker, core-mat fiberglass material to correct this problem.

When comparing construction methods, judge each

manufacturer and boat individually. Don't be taken in by broad claims of the superiority of one method of construction over another.

Molded Polyethylene: Introduced in 1983, with the arrival of the Aquaterra Chinook, polyethylene sea kayaks have steadily grown in popularity. Heavier, but less expensive and more rugged than their fiberglass or folding counterparts, poly boats are excellent entry-level sea kayaks.

The hulls and decks of polyethylene kayaks are created as a single unit through a process known as rotomolding. Pellets of plastic are introduced into a heated, metal mold which is then rocked and rotated, distributing an even layer of plastic throughout the surface of the mold. Unlike white water kayaks, which are made of cross-linked polyethylene, most poly sea kayaks are made of linear polyethylene. The linear material is more rigid and easier to repair.

The great expense involved in producing the molds has limited the designs of poly sea kayaks to those that will appeal to the largest potential markets. As a result, poly sea kayaks do not offer as great a variety of designs and levels of performance as can be found in fiberglass boats.

Folding: Folding boats have long been the mainstay of paddlers with a wanderlust. They have amply proven their toughness and seaworthiness on expeditions throughout the world, including the first trans-Atlantic crossing by kayak, more than 60 years ago.

Of all modern kayaks, folding kayaks are most reminscent of aboriginal wood and skin craft. They are built of a waterproof fabric skin stretched over a rigid frame of wood or tubular aluminium. The most common hull fabric is hypalon, a tough synthetic rubber. Decks are cotton or cordura nylon. The boats are much beamier than hardshell kayaks and the cockpits are quite large. For flotation and safety, air sponsons are located along the sides.

Folding boats range in weight from 30 pounds for a single to 90 pounds for a double. A K-1 will pack into a single bag the size of a large suitcase, but such portability comes at a price: folding boats are the most expensive of all

Figure 2   The Parts of a Sea Kayak

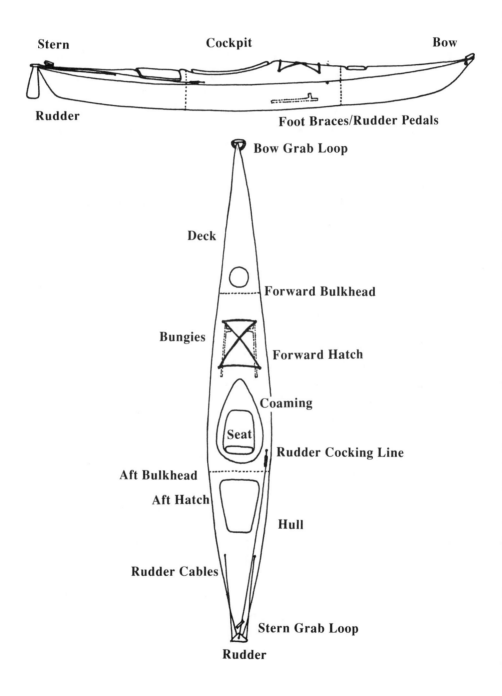

sea touring kayaks, ranging from \$2,500 for a single to \$4,000 for a top-of-the-line double.

Inflatable: Inflatable kayaks are gaining in acceptance and popularity, especially in the warm waters of the tropical Pacific where their transportability, seaworthiness and ability to bounce through hard landings are important features. The best are made of a tough nylon of polyester fabric coated with the plastic polyvinyl chloride, or hypalon. Inflatables are typically divided into several of air compartments: three major ones located in each side and the bottom and smaller ones located in the bow, stern and seats. The boats gain their rigidity from the two to four pounds per square inch of air pressure that inflates them. Weights range from 20 to 50 pounds and prices range from under \$200 to over \$1,000.

Features

Rudders: A rudder is a flat bladed steering apparatus controlled by a pair of foot pedals. Two cables, one for each pedal, run from the pedals to the rudder and allow the paddler to rotate the blade right and left on a fixed point set in the stern of the kayak. It is also hinged to lift up and slip over seaweed and other obstructions while the boat is moving forward in the water. A line is used to cock the rudder up and out of the way during transport, launching and landing, and backing over obstructions.

Rudders, although available as an option on nearly every boat made today, have been a subject of dispute among sea kayaking "experts" for years. Most either love them or hate them. Those that favor rudders cite improved paddling efficiency and the ease of hands-free maneuverability. Paddling purists point to rudders as another piece of equipment that can fail and as a device that lessens the paddlers reliance on basic paddling skills.

Over the years, improved designs, incorporating tougher materials and construction, have greatly increased the dependability of rudders. This improvement in reliability has made the advantages of a rudder far outweigh any disadvantages. In a cross-wind, a rudder allows the paddler to maintain a course with a minimum of wasted energy spent in corrective strokes, enabling the paddler to devote his or her energies to propulsion rather than position.

A rudder is indispensible to anyone taking photographs or fishing from a kayak. I would strongly recommend that a first-time boat buyer purchase a kayak with a rudder. You'll have an opportunity to try it both ways. If you don't like it, you can always leave it cocked out of the water.

Hatches: Hatches allow easy access through the deck to gear stored inside the boat, allowing bulky items such as camera cases and sleeping bags to be easily stowed and retrieved. Some feel that hatches invite disaster by compromising the waterproof integrity and strength of a solid deck, but as in the case of rudders, this objection has largely been overcome by improved designs.

Generally, smaller hatches are more watertight and more dependable than larger hatches. Look for secure and easy to operate closures and hatch designs that offer a positive seal through the use of a durable gasket. Never assume that a hatch is waterproof.

Bulkheads: Bulkheads are watertight walls that divide sections of a hard shell kayak's interior into compartments. They provide discrete areas for stowing gear and, much like the watertight compartments on larger boats, offer some measure of improved safety by providing buoyancy in case of capsize.

Do not assume that a bulkhead alone will keep your unprotected gear dry or provide enough buoyancy to keep your boat afloat in the event of a capsize. Be on the safe side: in addition to bulkheads use adequate flotation in the form of watertight gear bags of inflatable buoyancy bags.

Bulkheads are usually made of fiberglass/resin sheet glassed in place or rigid closed-cell foam secured with a flexible adhesive. You'll usually find bulkheads aft of the seat and forward of the foot braces.

Seats: Of all the features of a kayak, the seat is probably the single most troublesome—correct seat designs are as varied as the bottoms and backs they're supposed to fit. Fortunately, the seat is also the easiest feature to replace or adapt to your individual needs. Ideally, a kayak seat should provide a low center of gravity while lifting the paddler enough to make the position of the legs comfortable for long periods of time. Adequate lumbar support should be provided by the seat back without interfering with motion. The overall feel should be comfortable, with a secure feel for the boat.

If you find that the seat needs to be adapted to your contours, use sections of closed-cell foam like that found in backpacking sleeping pads. It can usually be glued in place with a waterproof adhesive or attached with duct tape.

Selecting a Kayak

When to buy: If you're a novice paddler, you should gain as much experience as possible through classes and on-the-water time in rentals before deciding to purchase a boat. You're ability to judge the feel of a kayak will be largely dependent on your experience and skill level. As your skills and confidence increase, so will your ability to discern the qualities of a boat's performance. Remember that the best choice is your choice, but you must be sure that you're making an informed decision.

Which Model: The first question that any prospective boat buyer should consider is: "What will I *really* use the boat for?" In the highly subjective world of kayak design, there are a great variety of boats available, each defining the needs of the sea kayaker a little differently. If you'll be using the boat for exclusively for day trips or fitness paddling, space for gear is not an issue. But if you plan to go on long distance tours, a high volume boat becomes a necessity. If you're an avid photographer or fisherman, stability is important. If most of your trips will involve travel by air, or if you lack storage for a hardshell boat, an inflatable or folding boat should be considered. If you'll be paddling exclusively in warm water, a open cockpit boat is an option. If you have an athletic bent and an interest in adventurous paddling, a narrow sport boat might be your best choice. If you're single, a K-1 is your best choice, but if you'll be paddling with your spouse or children, you might consider a K-2.

The answers to this question depends largely on your location, your interests, and your skill level. When examining how you will use your kayak, try to answer as honestly as you can. One of the common errors of first-time boat buyers is to choose the type of boat suited to their long-term goals, but not their present needs. Don't get a folding boat now because you plan to visit Crete someday. Don't get a narrow and demanding sport boat if it's unlikely that you'll have the time or the interest to develop the paddling skills it requires.

At the Store: After you've defined how you'll use your boat, it's time to try a few on. To further narrow the field, visit your dealer's sales floor. Select the boats that meet your basic needs. Take an inventory of features, and look at materials, workmanship and prices.

Now, climb in and get a feel for the fit. Is the cockpit large enough or small enough to accomodate you comfortably? Is there adequate foot room? Will the deck height and seat postion allow adequate elbow clearance? Can you firmly brace your knees? Does the seat feel snug and supportive? If the boat feels right, rent one.

On the Water: Until you've had a chance to be in the boat for at least a few hours, you have no way of knowing if its fit and feel is to your liking. Your dealer should have a selection of showroom models available for rental. To try out a wider variety than most dealers have on hand, visit a sea kayaking symposium (see Appendix V for locations).

Any decision regarding a boat purchase will involve compromise. No one kayak design can incorporate all of the desirable features, but with a little time and patience you can find a boat with the combination of features that is best suited for your needs.

2. GEAR

Paddle

The paddle is your propulsion, steering and stabilizer. You'll have it in your hands nearly all of time you're in your boat. And in the course of even a brief trip, you'll move the paddle through countless strokes. Next to your kayak, a paddle is the most important and personal piece of gear you'll purchase.

Materials: Sea touring paddles are available in a wide variety of materials in a number of combinations, including: vinylester, polyester and epoxy resins; fiberglass, graphite, kevlar, injection-molded plastic and wood. Materials determine the paddle's strength, weight, durability and cost.

Blade Shapes: The use of molded composites has allowed designers great freedom in shaping paddle blades. The best paddles balance various shapes to give the paddler the best combination of efficiency and stability.

Rounded blades reduce flutter.

Asymmetrical blades have less blade surface on the portion of the blade below the line of the shaft. As the blade enters and

moves through the water at an angle, torque is reduced by exposing each half of the blade face to equal amounts of pressure. This balances the load along the centerline of the blade face, reducing stress on the wrist and forearm and improving paddling efficiency.

Aleut styled paddles have long narrow blade faces that create less flutter (rapid side-to-side twisting motion of the blade), less resistance and less strain of wrists, forearms and shoulders. They have slow acceleration, but cruising speeds are easily maintained. They are also less suceptible to wind.

Figure 3   Paddle Shapes

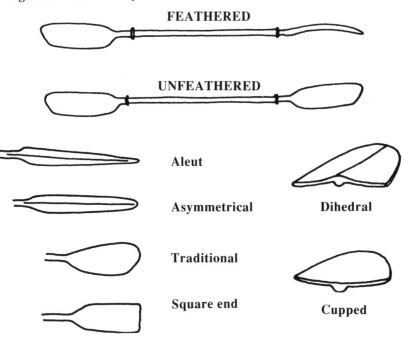

Wide blade faces create greater resistance during the power stroke. They are powerful and provide quick acceleration, but can cause a higher degree of stress on wrists arms and shoulders, particularly in heavy doubles.

Dihedral blades help reduce flutter and sideways slipage of the paddle by encouraging the water to flow off both halves of the blade face evenly.

Spooned blades provide more power by holding the water, but increase flutter.

Weight: The most expensive paddles--those that require particular attention during production and incorporate such space-age materials as graphite--are nearly always also the lightest in weight. These paddles can weigh under two pounds. The average weight of sea touring paddles is just over two and one half pounds, with the heaviest paddles tipping the scales at around three pounds. A weight range of little more than a pound may at first seem an inconsequential difference, and little justification for a price increase of as much as 100%, but after several thousand paddle strokes during a long trip the ounces can begin to count very heavily. Purchase the lightest paddle that your budget and anticipated hours of use will justify.

What Length? There is no formula for selecting the correct length of paddle. Beyond a few basic considerations, it's a matter of personal preference. The most common length for a general touring paddle is between seven to eight feet, ranging up to a maximum of nine feet. The best paddle for you is one suited to your size and strength and the size and handling of your boat. Remember that beamier boats often require longer paddles and narrow boats often require shorter paddles. Longer paddles require slow and powerful strokes. Shorter paddles demand a faster paddling cadence, but provide smoother acceleration.

Feathered or Unfeathered? A feathered paddle has blades rotated at at an angle on the axis of the shaft. An unfeathered paddle has its blades on the same plane.

There is endless debate about the advantages and disadvantages of feathered and unfeathered paddles, and any paddler you ask will probably have a strong opinion. Feathered blades offer less resistence to a head-wind, while unfeathered blades are best in a wind from the side. Unfeathered blades also require less wrist and forearm motion and are less likely to cause tendinitis. Each type works well under different circumstances and neither is best for all conditions. If you're a novice paddler, I suggest that you not enter the fray—try both by using a two-piece breakdown paddle and stick with the one that feels best to you. Or side-step the issue entirely by using an Aleut styled paddle that can be used only in the unfeathered position.

Accessories

Spray Skirt: The spray skirt is a watertight barrier that seals around your abdomen and the boat's coaming to keep water from entering the boat through the cockpit.

Spray skirts are made out of neoprene wetsuit material or coated nylon fabric. The rubber material is flexible, it stretches taught over the coaming and gives a snug fit around your waist, forming a positive seal and a smooth surface that easily sheds water. Coated nylon provides greater ventilation and a more comfortable fit. It won't stretch, so it is not as snug and will tend to pool water. Some models use both materials—neoprene to stretch over the coaming and nylon fabric around the paddlers abdomen—taking advantage of the best qualities of each.

Life Jacket: A life jacket or PFD (personal flotation device) is an essential part of every kayakers outfit. Life jackets designed for sea touring are certified by the U.S. Coast Guard, and must provide a minimum of 15.5 pounds of flotation. They are constructed of a nylon shell filled with vertical sections of closed-cell foam. Life jackets intended for general boating are not appropriate for kayaking, their long waists interfere with the spray skirt. Life jackets intended for kayaking are cut like a high vest, secured with a front zipper and a tie or snugging straps near the bottom.

The twofold role of a life jacket is simple: In case of a capsize, it holds your head above water so that you can breathe, and it enables you to float at the surface without expending precious energy. To do this, the life jacket must be in the right place at the right time—on you when you go in the water. A comfortable fit is very important. Look for a size that is fairly snug, but will allow adequate layers of clothing for the conditions you will typically encounter while paddling. The fit around your arms should allow ample room for movement.

Waterproof Bags: Waterproof bags are available in both coated nylon and PVC materials. Roll-down closures are the easiest to execute and provide the most dependable seals. PVC bags are generally more durable than nylon, and are widely available in a variety of sizes and weights.

When purchasing waterproof PVC gear bags, look for quality materials. The strength of PVC bags is in the thread—the vinyl only provides the seal. The fiber scrim of nylon or polyester gives a bag its tensile strength and puncture resistance. Less expensive PVC fabrics have a lower thread count, indicated by the larger gaps in the screen-like pattern of the underlying threads. PVC bags have two sides--a textured "scrim" side and a smooth "face" side. To check thread count, examine the scrim side.

The material's thickness, combined with denier and thread count, is the best indication of the fabric's overall ability to withstand abrasion, punctures, cutting and tearing. Heavier, stiffer materials do not fold as tightly and will not form as reliable a seal in a standard roll-down closure as a lighter weight fabric. Weight works against the "hand" of the material—generally, the heavier the material, the stiffer its feel—so you must usually compromise between the bag's watertightness and durability.

Flotation: Flotation is essential to safety in the event of a capsize. On a long trip, flotation can be provided by a boat-load gear stowed in waterproof bags. For shorter trips, bouyancy bags are the answer. These contoured nylon or plastic inflatable bags fit into the boat's bow and stern.

Bailers, Pumps & Sponges: A small bleach bottle with its bottom and part of one side cut away works well for routine bailing when you've got a few quarts of water sloshing around inside the cockpit (it's also handy when nature calls and a landing is inconvenient). Small high volume hand pumps that move water at a rate of seven to 12 gallons per minute are necessary for emergency bailing following a capsize. Battery powered electric pumps are also available.

A large sponge like those commonly found in marine supply and specialty kayaking stores are handy for sopping up the last remnants of water and for general cleaning.

Whistle or Air Horn: A waterproof whistle or a compact compressed air horn provide clear, loud, and distinctive means of signaling other members of your party.

Waterproof Flashlight: My favorite is a three-cell high-intensity diver's flashlight with an attached stainless steel ring and spring-loaded clip.

Paddle Leash: A leash will keep a wayward paddle where you need it—within reach. Use a four to five foot line tied to a cleat near the front of the cockpit and attached to your paddle

Towline: A towline—at least 50 feet of parachute cord—should be a part of every paddler's basic gear.

Emergency Signal Kit: Emergency signals have one purpose: To attract attention and indicate your location in the event of an emergency that requires rescue or prompt medical attention. Every kayaker should carry a set of emergency signals and be familiar with their most effective use.

A basic kit would contain:

>2 parachute flares
>1 pack of 3 "pocket" aerial flares
>1 smoke canister
>1 strobe light.

Weather radio: Handy for day trips and indispensable on long tours, inexpensive pocket weather radios will provide you with current conditions and forecasts from National Oceanic and Atmospheric Administration weather stations.

Clothing

In temperate areas comfort and safety mean staying dry and, if you do get wet, it means staying warm. Rule one is to avoid cotton. Stick to materials that insulate when wet—wool or synthetics. Rule two is to select clothing that is adaptable.

Use the fewest items that will accommodate the greatest range of conditions. This can best be accomplished through layering.

Your lower body is held within the nearly airtight confines of the kayak, sealed with a spray skirt and surrounded by still air. It requires the least attention. In warmer weather, quick drying shorts are adequate. In cooler weather, a pair of long underwear bottoms or bunting pants work well.

In a kayak, your upper body experiences the greatest range of temperatures and conditions. It's exposed to the elements and will loose and gain heat through a variety of mechanisms, from heat loss through convection (wind) to heat gain through work (paddling). You can use your clothing to regulate the temperature and maintain a comfortable range.

Layer One—Vapor Transmission: This is the layer next to your skin and its role is to lessen evaporative cooling by transmitting moisture to the next layer. Snug-fitting underwear, made of non-absorbent plastic fibers such as polypropylene or polyester, is your best choice. Look for a lightweight fabric intended for active use.

Layer Two—Insulation: This layer traps and holds air warmed by your body. Pile or bunting is your best choice. Avoid collars, cuffs or hems made of absorbent knit.

Layer Three—Shell: This layer shields you from wind and water. Without it, the effectiveness of the two previous layers is greatly reduced. Breathable/waterproof fabrics do not work effectively when exposed to salt water, so your best choice is a coated waterproof material. Avoid open cuffs, they allow water to run down your arms as you paddle. There are a number of waterproof shells designed specifically for sea kayaking that offer features such as neoprene cuff and neck closures, functional hoods and handy pockets positioned to clear the top of your spray skirt.

Ventilation is important to the functioning of the other layers—you must have a way to effectively vent accumulating heat and moisture. Unfortunately, ventilation compromises waterproofness. It's a trade-off. A paddling jacket that lets air out *will* let water in, but it will also be more comfortable in the majority of paddling situations.

In the hot summer weather or the tropics, coolness and protection from the sun are your greatest concerns. A long sleeved cotton shirt paired with quick-drying shorts will work well. The cotton fabric will accumulate salt quickly and develop a greasy feel if it isn't periodically rinsed in fresh water. A light windshell will provide protection from cool breezes on an off the water and a pair of light cotton pants will make for comfortable morning and evening beach attire.

Head: If your rain shell doesn't have an adequate hood, a sou-wester style rain hat works well. Its brim will channel dripping water away from your face and out of your field of vision. Select a size large of enough to accommodate a wool or synthetic fleece cap.

For sunny weather, a wide-brimmed cotton hat with a chin-tie for windy weather will prevent sun hitting both your face and the back of your neck. On particularly warm days, cool your head by dipping the hat in the water before putting it on.

Your head can account for up to one-half of your body's total heat loss. In cold water, where there is a chance of capsize, or when practicing rolls and rescues, adequate insulative head wear is important to your comfort and safety. The neoprene caps, like those used by white water boaters, or full neoprene hoods should be worn.

Hands: For cold weather paddling nothing can beat the warmth, convenience and direct hand-to-paddle contact of pogies. These mitt-like hand covers are made of neoprene or waterproof nylon with a liner made of synthetic fleece. The assembled units open to slip over the paddle shaft and secure with velcro closures. You simply slip your hands inside and grab the paddle shaft.

In sunny weather, the outer fabric shells of pogies make great sun protection for the backs of your hands--a place very susceptible to sunburn while paddling.

Feet: In warm climates, sandals that fit securely and will stay in place in the water are your best choice. My favorites have durable and supportive rubber foot beds, mid-soles and soles with nylon webbing straps and plastic snaps. Another

warm weather choice is a pair of "tabis," slip-on fabric shoes
with tough, no-slip soles. They are readily available in Hawaii
and can be found on the mainland at many Asian markets.

Cold water paddlers generally prefer waterproof rubber or
plastic "farm" boots. Combined with a wool sock, they provide
the best combination of warmth, comfort and dryness. Their
biggest drawback is bulk—larger sizes will often not fit in the
limited space of a kayak and still allow full movement of
rudder pedals. Another choice is neoprene booties. They
provide warmth and, with a durable sole, protection from rocks
while wading, but are uncomfortable to wear for long periods.

Wet suits and Dry suits: A wet suit or drysuit will provide
thermal protection in case of a capsize in cold water or while
practicing recoveries. Either can be worn as a precaution
during crossings. The most popular wet suits for sea touring
are one-eighth inch neoprene farmer john style wet suit (full
body and legs, no sleeves). Dry suits are considerably more
expensive than wet suits, but offer greater comfort and warmth.

3. PADDLE TECHNIQUES

Paddle Brace Entry/Exit

This simple technique (Figure 4) will provide you with a stable base while getting in and out of the kayak on calm beaches. Set the boat in shallow water parallel to the beach. On the shore side of the boat, face the bow, squat next to the cockpit and lay your paddle behind you across the deck. The paddle shaft should be perpendicular to the line of the boat, touching the outer edge of the coaming. The blade on the shore side should rest on a flat and secure surface. Reach behind and grab the shaft with your shore-side hand and firmly grab the coaming and paddle shaft with your water-side hand. Shift your weight evenly on to both hands and step into the boat by first sitting on the back section of the coaming, then carefully sliding your feet forward to the footbraces and your butt into the seat.

Figure 4   Paddle Brace entry/Exit

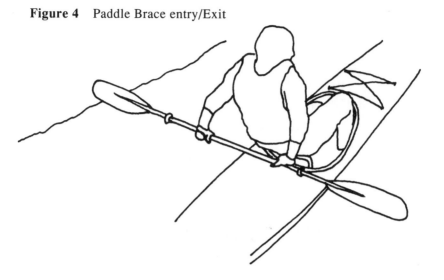

Dock or Pool Entry/Exit

The paddle brace entry is also suitable for docks, floats, pool edges and other platforms that are no higher than your boat's coaming. It is essentially the same sequence of movements as the beach entry, except instead of squatting next to the boat you begin by sitting along the edge of the platform with your feet forward.

Figure 5   Dock or Pool Entry/Exit

Figure 6

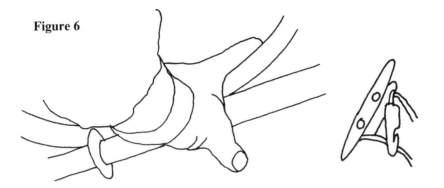

The Paddle Stroke

Hold the paddle loosely with your hands comfortably spaced at about shoulder width. Sit with a straight back and brace with your knees and your feet. Center your balance in your hips and let your lower body sense the motion of the boat while you use your back, shoulders and abdomen—not your arms—to pull through the stroke. To begin your stroke with your left blade, bring your left shoulder forward while almost straightening your left arm. Do not bend forward. Reach forward with the paddle and slide the blade into the water close to the hull of the boat (Figure 7-A). Grip the paddle loosely and pull with the lower (left) hand while pushing out with the upper (right) hand. Keep your hands below eye-level and don't cross the centerline with the hand (right) that is pushing the paddle forward (Figure 7-B). Apply steady force through the first half of the stroke, rotating your shoulders and keeping your wrists in the neutral position. (Your hand should extend in line with your forearm, not angled up or down.) (Figure 7-C). Just as your knees are even with the blade in the water, lessen the force applied to the paddle. Continue moving your right shoulder forward as you follow through the stroke. Lift the left blade from the water behind you and begin the second half of the cycle by reaching forward with the right blade (Figure 7-D).

The closer your paddle blade moves along the centerline of the boat, the more efficient your forward motion will be. Increase the outward sweep to increase stability.

To move backwards, simply reverse the motion, using shorter strokes and the backs of the paddle blades.

Figure 7   Paddle Stroke Sequence

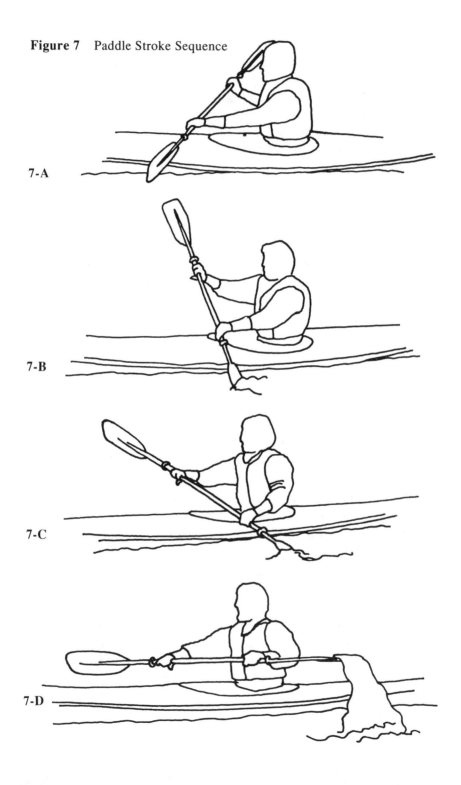

7-A

7-B

7-C

7-D

Sweep Stroke

To make a correction in your course while under way or to turn the boat when maneuvering in close quarters, use a *sweep stroke* (Figure 8). Begin as you would for a basic paddle stroke on the side opposite the direction you want to turn. Instead of pushing forward with your upper hand, bring it across to the center-line close to your chest as your lower hand pulls the blade in a wide shallow arc.

Figure 8   Sweep Stroke

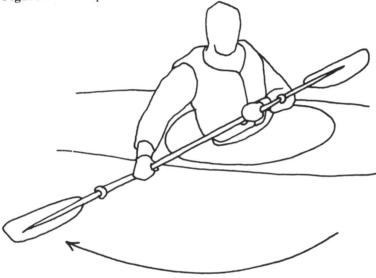

Draw Stroke

The *draw stroke* (Figure 9) moves you sideways. Twist and face the side in the direction that you want to move and extend the paddle out as far as you comfortably can while holding it in a near vertical position. Plant the blade in the water and draw the boat to the paddle. As your boat approaches the blade, swing the blade from the water by bringing your upper hand down to the front, using your lower hand as a pivot. Be careful to not let the boat overtake the submerged paddle blade.

Figure 9 Draw Stroke

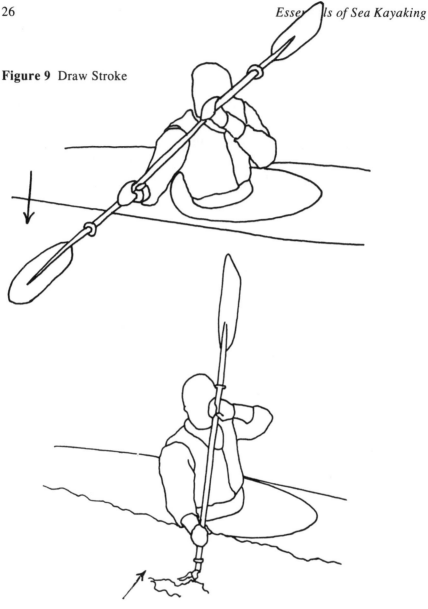

Bracing

Bracing is one of the most important basic paddling skills. A brace will help you avoid capsize and maintain stability in a variety of conditions. Bracing should be a reflexive extension of your paddle stroke. Use a high brace during the first half of your stroke and a low brace during the last half.

Low Brace: Interrupt your stroke and quickly move the paddle to the neutral position—centered in front of you, level with the water and perpendicular to the boat—just above deck height. Immediately slide it to the bracing side until your outside hand (opposite the bracing side) is even with your navel. Slap the back of the blade flat against the surface of the water as you apply a quick downward push with your inside arm. As you recover, and downward force is no longer exerted on the now submerged blade, quickly rotate it 90 degrees to pull it cleanly from the water. Bring the paddle back to the neutral position where another brace can be executed if needed.

Figure 10   Low Brace

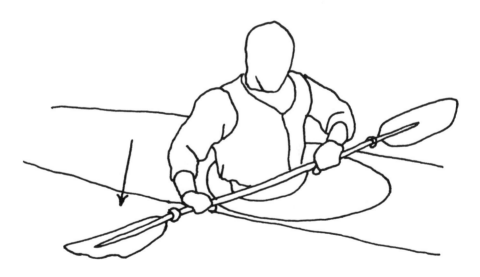

High Brace: From your paddle stroke, quickly bring the paddle to the neutral position about chin-high. Shift it to the bracing side until your outside hand is next to your outside cheek and your forearm is vertical. This will bring the face of the blade on the bracing side into a position parallel with the surface of the water. (Unlike the low brace, the high brace uses the face of blade.) With both wrists straight, bring the inside arm down as you hold your outside hand stationary and below eye level, with the elbow close to your body. Hit the water at a point between your hip and knee. Disengage as you would for a low brace by rotating the paddle and returning to a neutral position.

Figure 11   High Brace

4. SAFETY

Sea kayaking safety is an individual matter that affects the safety of the entire party. Each paddler must take responsibility for his or her own well-being, assessing the risk involved in any action and deciding if the risk is acceptable.

To properly appraise risk you must be able to perceive and evaluate the given situation. This puts the novice paddler at a disadvantage—without experience you cannot make a prudent judgement. *Act conservatively until you've gained experience and your skills are well established.*

1. Know Your Limits: Be honest with yourself and your companions about your experience and skill level. Stay out of any situation that is beyond your capabilities unless it is a controlled learning situation with experienced paddlers at hand. Do not attempt open crossings until you have mastered capsize prevention and recovery techniques. Do not paddle alone.

2. Communicate with your companions: Never hesitate to speak up if you feel uncomfortable with a planned route or if you feel developing conditions are beyond your skills.

3. Develop your paddling skills: Braces should be repeated until they are a matter of reflex. Recoveries should be practiced, practiced, practiced—under safe, but difficult, "real-water" conditions.

4. Plan your trip: Carefully plan your route, including landing sites and potential emergency pull-outs, before you leave the beach.

5. Practice proper group organization: Realistically appraise the skill level of the paddlers in your group. Base decisions on the skills of the weakest paddler. Keep group sizes small—no more than eight or ten paddlers. Use the buddy system and keep all paddlers within ear-shot.

6. Be properly outfitted: All members of your paddling party should be properly outfitted. That means that each paddler should:

Wear a life vest

Carry his or her own rescue, emergency and navigation equipment

Have adequate buoyancy in both bow and stern

Be properly clothed and have extra clothing handy

7. Know the paddling environment: Anticipate and avoid dangerous situations. Be aware of weather, winds, tides, currents and coastal hazards.

Recoveries

Recovery skills are best learned through hands-on experience with the supervision and support of an experienced teacher. Once learned, these are skills that all sea kayakers, novice and expert alike, must frequently practice. Pool practice is limited in its applicability to real situations—you'll rarely need to recover from a capsize in warm, calm water.

The best practice sites are near-shore locations that will provide real conditions. Care must be taken to insure that the practice remains a practice, not a rescue. **Good sense, good planning and adequate support are necessities.**

Assisted Recovery

If you're the rescuer: Pull alongside and right the victim's capsized kayak. Take the paddle from the victim and place it with your paddle across your lap. With the paddles secured beneath your arms and chest, extending from your lap across the victim's boat, reach across and grab the victim's bow coaming with the nearest hand. Hold the far back quarter of the victim's coaming with the other hand. Pull the boats together and create a stable platform by distributing your weight evenly between them.

If you're the victim: Hang on to your paddle as you exit the boat. Approach your boat from the side opposite the rescuer and face the cockpit. Hand the rescuer your paddle. After the rescuer is in position, reach up, grab the back and near sides of the coaming. Pull your upper body up onto the deck behind the cockpit. Stay low and reach with the near hand to the rescuer's boat for added support. Bring the leg closest to the rescuer up and into the cockpit. Slide toward the bow, bringing your other leg up and into the cockpit just before you turn and slip your hips into the cockpit. Bail or pump the water from your boat

Figure 12   Assisted Recovery

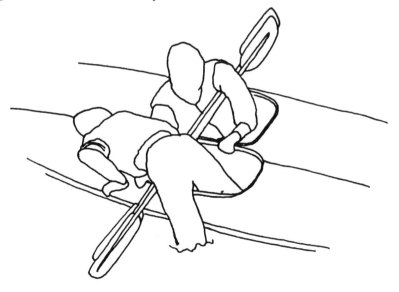

Figure 13   Loop Recovery

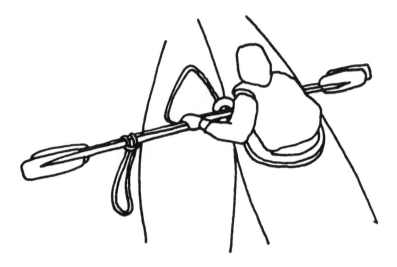

Loop Recovery

This recovery uses a three-eighths inch diameter polypropylene rope tied into a loop five to seven feet long.

If you're the rescuer: Pull alongside and right the victim's kayak. Take the paddle from the victim and attach the loop to both paddles in a stirrup as illustrated in Figure 13. Place the paddles across your lap and behind the the coaming of the victim's boat. Grip the paddles at the coaming with the hand on the aft side of the victim's boat while holding the close side of the coaming with your other hand. Lean across the paddles and hold them firmly wedged beneath your chest and armpit. As the victim enters the kayak, push or lift on the coaming to compensate for the boat's movement.

If you're the victim: Hang on to your paddle as you exit the boat. Approach your boat from the side and face the cockpit. Hand the rescuer your paddle. After the rescuer has attached the loop and posiitioned the paddles, grab the paddles with the hand on the aft side and place either foot in the stirrup with the other.

Keep your hand on the paddle and grab the back of the coaming with the other. Pull yourself up, using your leg for support, face-down onto the paddle and the deck behind the cockpit. Stay low and reach with the near hand to the rescuer's boat for added support. Slip your foot into the cockpit. As soon as your weight is removed from the loop there will be a loss of stability. Both rescuer and victim must be careful to maintain balance. Bring the other foot up and into the cockpit, then slide toward the bow, turning so that your hips slip into the cockpit. Bail or pump the water from your boat.

Hypothermia

This deadly condition, caused by the lowering of your body's core temperature to below 95 degrees Fahrenheit, is responsible for more sea-kayaking deaths than any other cause. In fact, many fatalities attributed to drowning are the direct result of hypothermia. Hypothermia can be divided into two types determined by the speed of the onset of the disease.

Chronic Hypothermia is the result of gradual heat loss over an extended period of time. It commonly occurs in cold, wet and windy weather where the victim is inadequately clothed and often unaware of his or her worsening condition.

Immersion Hypothermia is the result of rapid cooling caused by water's great ability to conduct heat. A victim in water will lose heat at a rate 20 times greater than in air of the same temperature. Many paddlers mistakenly assume that immersion hypothermia is a risk only in frigidly cold conditions, but it can occur in water as warm as 68 degrees Fahrenheit. Hypothermia can be prevented if adequate precautions are taken: Clothing should insulate when wet. Rainwear and extra clothing should be easily accessible from the cockpit. A wet suit, dry suit and neoprene hood or cap should be worn when there is a risk of capsize or during practice of recoveries.

Diagnosing and Treating Hypothermia: The symptoms of hypothermia are inconsistent and unpredictable. One of its effects is a loss of mental ability—you, several of your companions, or your entire party may become hypothermic and not be aware of it. Without adequate outwards signs to alert members of a paddling party, the first indication of a chronically hypothermic paddler may be a capsize. Chronic hypothermia is indicated if a paddler begins to exhibit confused, erratic, inattentive or sluggish behavior; slurred speech, or shivering. Immersion hypothermia should be assumed, whether symptoms are exhibited or not, following a capsize in cold water (55 degrees or lower) when the victim was not wearing a wet suit or dry suit or when there has been prolonged exposure.

To treat hypothermia:

1. Get the victim to shore as quickly as possible.
2. Handle the victim gently.
3. Remove wet clothing and replace with dry clothing or other dry covering.
4. Shelter the victim from wind and rain.
5. Insulate with a dry sleeping bag, parkas, or any other suitable material. Add moderate heat to head, neck, chest, and groin.
6. Provide something to drink. Do not give coffee or alcohol.
7. Place victim by a roaring fire or other heat source.
8. In severe cases have one, or preferably two, rescuers strip and join the naked victim in a large sleeping bag.

5. ON THE WATER

When you place your boat on the water you enter a changing world of tides, currents, wind and waves. Every sea kayaker should become well-acquainted with the watery environment where he or she paddles. In this chapter we look at fundamental skills for protected water paddling: understanding tides and currents, planning a trip and basic navigating.

Tides and Currents

Tides: Tides are a gravitational effect of the sun and moon. The moon, though it is considerably smaller than the sun, has a greater effect because it is much closer. The moon orbits around the earth once each 27 days, eight hours, creating

13 lunar cycles each year. As the earth rotates around the sun, a particular longitudinal meridian is affected by the moon's gravitational pull every 24 hours and 50 minutes. The resulting periodic bulge of water—the tide—follows several hours after the passage of the moon.

Tide height is the up and down motion of water drawn toward the moon. The average of the lower low tides—the mean low water—at a particular reference point is indicated as 0.0. A *minus tide*, indicated as -0.1 or lower, is below the average lower low tide for that location. A *high tide*, indicated by 0.1 or more is greater than the average lower low tide for that location. The vertical distance between the highest and lowest tides is called the *tide range*.

Tides create a constantly changing topography as the waters alternately cover and expose the shore. A suitable landing site that lies within yards of a campsite at high tide, might mean a long hike on an exposed beach at low tide. Careful consideration of tides must accompany all decisions regarding landing and camp sites.

Currents: As the water cycles through the up and down motion of the tides, it also moves in and out—these are the *tidal currents*. A tidal current flowing into a coastal embayment is called the *flood*; when it moves out, it is called the *ebb*. The period between ebb and flow, when there is no movement of the water, is called *slack water*. The strength of a current is dependent on the size of the tide—the volume of water that is being moved—and the shape of the landform through which the water must move. As the current cycles from slack to ebb or flood, it builds to a maximum speed, known as maximum ebb or maximum flood.

Currents can be both a help and a hazard for paddlers. The hydraulics created by the combination of rapidly moving water over rugged bottom contours or through narrow passages can create very dangerous conditions, and the steep waves formed by winds moving against the direction of the current's flow can be a hazard. Both situations should be approached only at slack water. On the other hand, currents can be a great help when you plan your route through safe waters with the direction of the flow. Current tables and charts should be used to predict the time, direction and volume of flow for any given area.

If you do find yourself moving against the current, position your kayak close to shore where the flow of water is the weakest.

Trip Planning

Planning is essential to every kayak trip—even a lunch-hour outing. You must determine how much time you have for the trip, the distance to be traveled and how long it will take. A safe route must be selected. Tides, currents, wind, and weather must be taken into account. Possible landing and campsites must be considered.

A touring kayak with an average paddler will move at a comfortable cruising speed of between two to three knots. For an enjoyable day trip, plan nothing more than three to four hours paddling time, about eight nautical miles roundtrip. When figuring distances and times for longer trips, accounting for stops, weather, rest days, and other delays, plan on a conservative average of about eight nautical miles per day. By that standard, a seven day trip could comfortably cover 56 miles. If your party took two rest days, that would leave five travel days at an average of just over 11 miles—about five hours paddling time—per day.

Navigation

Kayak navigation begins with a carefully planned route. After that comes the disarmingly simple sounding task of keeping track of where you are and where you want to go. It can be as easy as sighting various landmarks along a sunny shore and locating them on your chart or as challenging as executing an open water crossing well out of sight of land. This book offers a cursory look at the tools of kayak navigation for near-shore travel in protected waters. The skills and techniques needed for open coast paddling and open water crossings are beyond the range of any novice and beyond the scope of this book. For a more in-depth treatment of kayak navigation, I strongly recommend that you read *Fundamentals of Kayak Navigation*, by David Burch (see Appendix 2).

Navigation Tools

Nautical Charts: Charts of U.S. waters are published by the National Ocean Survey (NOS), a department of the National Oceanographic and Atmosphereic Administration (NOAA). Charts of Canadian waters are available from the Canadian Hydrographic Service (see Appendix 4). Nautical charts provide the kayaker with invaluable information about coastal features and are essential to navigation. Depth readings (soundings) are indicated numerically in fathoms (three feet), shoreline tidal range is indicated by color, and symbols are used to indicate shoreline composition and obstructions. Navigation aids, such as buoys and lights, and landforms and others features visible from the water, are also indicated by symbols.

Every beginning navigator should first acquire the pamphlet titled *Chart No. 1.* This key to the meanings of chart chart symbols is available at most chart dealers.

Generally, novice kayakers should use the most detailed chart for the area they will be paddling. This means the chart with the largest scale—1:20,000 (one inch on the chart equals 20,000 inches of the area mapped) or larger. Remember that the scale increases as the second number decreases. A 1:40,000 chart is less detailed than a 1:20,000 chart.

To locate the charts for an area you plan to visit, you will need the NOAA Nautical Chart Catalog for the region. Select the chart by consulting the catalog's coverage diagram and the accompanying list indicating the name, number and scale of each chart shown. Each catalog also includes the addresses of authorized chart dealers in the region.

Chart case: A clear plastic chart case with a watertight seal serves two important uses—it keeps your charts dry and provides a means of securing your charts to the deck where it will be accessible without opening the spay skirt.

Tidal Current Charts and Tables: Also published by NOS, tidal current charts and tables show the direction and speed of tidal flow.

Tide Tables: Familiar to most ocean fishermen, tide tables indicate the times and heights of high and low water for various reference stations within a given area.

Topographic Maps: Nautical charts provide very limited landform information. United States Geological Survey topological maps are useful for selecting suitable sites for sheltering from winds, landing and camping.

Compass: You can use either a hand-held orienteering style compass or a more expensive, but more convenient, deck-mounted marine compass.

Dividers: Small dividers are used to accurately and easily measure distances on a chart.

Straight-edge: A small plastic ruler tethered to your chart case, or the edge of a hand held compass can be used to draw bearing lines.

Piloting

Every kayaking trip begins from a known point. As you move from that point you must keep track of your position. This can most easily be accomplished by *piloting*—a method of navigation familiar to anyone that has found their way through an unfamiliar city by using recognizable landmarks.

To navigate by piloting on water, you simply note landmarks on the shore (lights, headlands, etc.) or on the water (buoys and daymarks). Next, locate the landmark on the chart and identify your position on the water relative to the landmark.

A more precise means of noting your location is by using a *range.* A range is a line through two fixed points. If you draw a line along the headlands of two small islands, (Figure 14) you know that at the moment the closer island obscures the more distant island you are located along that line. This is called a *line of position.* An intersecting line drawn from another range or a compass reading off another landmark will indicate or *fix* your exact location.

To take the compass reading, aim the compass at the target. If you're using a deck-mounted compass, point the bow toward the target. Keep as steady as possible until an average reading can be established. This is your *bearing.* Draw a line along that bearing extending out from the target. If no ranges are available, two compass bearing lines can be used to fix your position.

Figure 14   Taking a Range

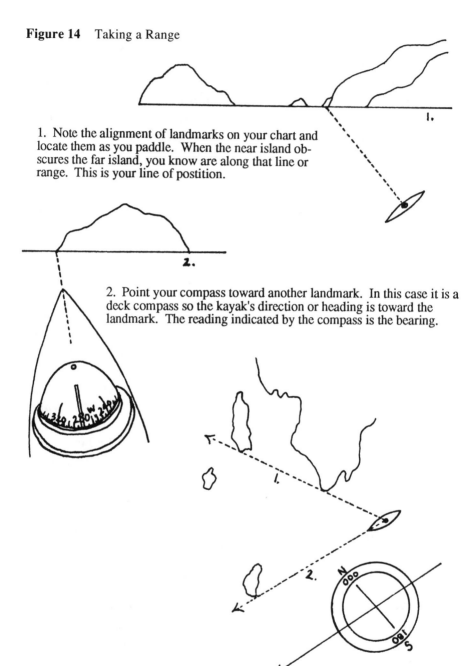

1. Note the alignment of landmarks on your chart and locate them as you paddle. When the near island obscures the far island, you know are along that line or range. This is your line of postition.

2. Point your compass toward another landmark. In this case it is a deck compass so the kayak's direction or heading is toward the landmark. The reading indicated by the compass is the bearing.

3. To find your extact position, mark the range and the bearing on your chart, the intersection is your location or fix.

Crossing a Current

Maintaining a specific course when crossing a current is not a consideration if your destination is simply the opposite shore of a long channel or a point well downstream of where you begin your crossing. In fact, if you want to make the quickest possible crossing to the opposite shore, in order to outrun weather or limit your exposure in the open water of the channel, your best choice is to simply paddle straight across and let the current move you downstream.

Maintaining your course when crossing becomes important if you must reach a specific point directly across on the opposite shore. If you simply launch and attempt to paddle directly to your destination, you will be swept sideways by the flow of water and away from your intended landing.

The technique used for the controlled crossing of a current is ferrying—angling your boat into the current so that you move from shore to shore along a predictable line. As you ferry across the channel, you will be paddling into the current and moving at a speed that is less than your actual paddling speed. You control the line of your crossing by orienting the angle of your forward direction and your paddling speed to compensate for the direction and speed of the water. Your paddling speed and the speed of the current will determine the correct angle. This is known as the ferry angle.

The simplest way to set the ferry angle and maintain a course across a current is to use a natural range (Figure 15). Houses, trees, large rocks, hills and other shoreline landmarks all make convenient targets. To establish your range, select two landmarks in line with your destination. The correct angle will be indicated by the relative positions of landmarks. Keep them in line and you're on course. Correct your speed and angle by adjusting to the positions of the landmarks. Once you've found the correct angle and speed, refer to your compass and note the heading or check the shore for additional landmarks that will remain visible and in line as you approach closer to your destination. Use these to maintain your course as you approach the shore.

It is wise to over-correct at the beginning of a crossing by heading slightly upstream of your destination. The current is likely to be fastest in the deeper water at the mid-point of the channel and a prudent beginning will allow greater room for error as the crossing proceeds.

When deciding where to cross, bear in mind that the current accelerates as a waterway narrows—the section of a channel with the shortest shore-to-shore span is not necessarily the best place to cross. A longer crossing through slower water may be a better choice.

Figure 15   Crossing a Current

1. Note the alignment of landmarks on the opposite shore. Select two in line with your destination.

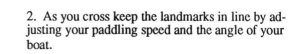

2. As you cross keep the landmarks in line by adjusting your paddling speed and the angle of your boat.

You should also consider what lies downstream. You should not cross at a location where there is a chance that you will be carried into open water, rips or other dangerous conditions.

When to cross depends largely on your route and the speed of the current. If you're traveling well downstream of a moderate current, you can plan to cross using the current for an additional push. When traveling across the channel to a specific point, you would ideally cross at slack water when the current is at its weakest. That window of time can be determined by using the NOAA Tidal Current Tables. You can also determine how long the current will move at a speed of less than   knot on each side of slack water by dividing 60 minutes by the peak current speed in knots.

6. PACKING AND LOADING

How you pack and load your gear is more than a matter of convenience—it will affect the safety of your journey and the seaworthiness of your boat. Important items such a extra clothing and emergency equipment must be easily accessible. Waterproof bags must be used to protect your gear from the damaging effects of water and to provide flotation in case of a capsize. And finally, your gear must be well-secured and distributed so that your boat will maintain proper balance.

Packing Your Gear

Store any items that would be damaged by contact with water in durable waterproof bags. These bags will not only keep your equipment dry, they will also provide added buoyancy. Your sleeping bag and spare clothing could be critical in a survival situation and should always be well protected from water.

Do not over-fill waterproof bags. Leave a little extra space so that the bags' material is not stretched taut. This will make the bag less prone to punctures (it will also be easier to fit in the boat). Pack your sleeping bag in its stuff sack and then slip it inside a roomy waterproof bag.

It's easier and safer to use a number of smaller bags than several large bags. The smaller bags allow for more efficient use of the boat's storage space, and their greater numbers mean your gear will suffer less damage from a single leak.

Take particular care when you fill and close roll-down bags—usually it's not the fabric that leaks, it's the seal. Fill the bags about two-thirds full and squeeze the air out. Fold the closure so that the material is smooth, with tight, crisp turns.

Organize your gear by use, just as you would if you were packing a backpack. Items that are used together should be packed together whenever possible. Separate food into several bags divided into rations for every few days.

Loading Your Boat

Trim is aboat's bow to stern balance in the water. Generally, it's best to adjust for level trim. But you may find that your boat handles more to your liking with the load slightly heavier toward the bow or stern.

A handy method of loading, taught by Lee Moyer of Seattle's Pacific Water Sports, is to divide your gear into four piles. The first pile consists of items that you want close at hand—water bottle, sunscreen, lunch, camera, rain gear, emergency equipment, etc. These should be set aside and loaded last. The remaining gear is divided by weight into three piles of equal size. One pile contains all of the heaviest items; one pile contains all of the lightest items and the last pile contains what's left. Set aside one or two of the heaviest smaller items to be loaded later as final trim adjustments. The remainder of the heavy items should be placed aft, close to the middle of the boat, with the heaviest items along the centerline. The medium weight pile should be stored in the forward part of the kayak. The light weight pile should be placed in the stern. Stow infrequently used items or gear that you won't need for a few days—spare spray skirt, repair kit, food for later in the trip—in the most inaccessible parts of the boat. The lightest of these items should go in the bow and stern (a line tied to bags will make removal easier).

Place your shelter—tent or tarp—along with your stove or fire starting materials, and the ingredients for your evening meal on top where they can be easily reached when you land.

Now load the items you want close-at-hand. These can be easily stored in a dry bag kept forward of the seat, between your legs.

On Deck

The deck is the place for gear that you want access to without opening your spray skirt or for awkward items that won't fit below. You should restrict your deck load to items that are lightweight, won't catch the wind, and won't be damaged by exposure to heat, sun, salt water and rain.

Your chart case and compass should be securely attached just forward of the cockpit. Small items can be kept in a small deck bag. Larger items, like your spare paddle or fishing rod should be securely tied to cleats with nylon line. Use shock-cord (bungies) only to keep things snug.

Carrying an Unloaded Kayak

First empty any water that might be inside the boat. Remove the hatches and with the help of another person positioned at the opposite end of the boat, lift it by grabbing the bow and stern and invert it so that the deck is facing the ground. Drain the water by first raising one end, then the other so that the water exits from the cockpit and hatch openings.

When two people are carrying the boat, simply use the grab loops located at the stern and bow. If you're alone, and fairly strong, you can carry the boat by lifting it up and resting the inside of the coaming on your shoulder. Balance the boat by positioning your shoulder at the boat's center of gravity and steadying the load with your free hand.

Another method, useful for long hauls or if your boat is too heavy or cumbersome to carry on your shoulder, is to use a small two-wheeled cart. The carts, available at most kayak dealers, attach to the boat's stern and allows you to roll your way between the car and the put-in.

Carrying a Loaded Kayak

The best practice is to avoid carrying a kayak when it's fully loaded—it's hazardous for both you and your boat.

If you must move a loaded boat, the best method I've found is the strap carry recommended by John Dowd, author of *Sea Kayaking: A Manual for Long Distance Touring.* You'll need two straps made of two inch nylon webbing four to eight feet long with grab-loops sewn at each end. When four people are present, run two straps under the boat, one at the bow and stern about three feet in from the end. This safely distributes the load without placing undue stress on any single area of the hull and allows the carriers to hoist the heavy load with their legs and not their backs.

If you are alone or with one other person, use a strap to lift one end of the boat at a time, walking it up the beach by rotating it 180 degrees with each turn.

7. GETTING THERE

Cartopping

I often feel that I put my kayak in the water just to wash the road grit off. Like most paddlers, my boat sees nearly as much road-time as water-time. Before you pull onto the highway for your first trip, here are a few things you should know:

Don't scrimp on racks, buy a quality set that locks securely to your car. Yakima and Thule top the list. They're sturdy, dependable and able to accommodate a variety of sporting equipment.

Locate the racks on your car so that the crossbars are as far apart as possible. If they're too close together, the boat will be less stable and most of its weight will be concentrated on one area of the hull.

Fiberglass kayaks should be placed right-side up with the hull resting on cradles. Polyethylene kayaks are best carried upside down with the deck resting on cradles so that any deformation will not misshape the hull and affect performance. When the boat is in the water, the deck will be heated by the sun and quickly return to its original shape.

Tie your boat securely—bow and stern to the bumpers and the hull to the rack crossbars. Use one quarter or five sixteenths solid braid nylon line. It holds knots better than polypropylene line and is easier to handle and more rot resistant than manila. Buy line in ten foot sections. Wait to trim the length until you're sure how you'll be rigging your rack.

Do not use elastic cord (bungies). It stretches too easily, allowing your boat to bounce and shift position. Make a habit of always tying your boat down as soon as it's placed on the rack and removing your boat as soon as it's untied. Many unsecured boats have been damaged when blown from racks by unexpected gusts of wind.

Use a *trucker's hitch* (Figure 16) for the snugging knots on all lines. To tie to the bumpers, run a line through the bumper and the grab-loop on the boat end. On one end of the rope, tie a loop. Run the free end of the line through the loop, pull tight and secure with a trucker's hitch.

To secure your boat to the cross bars, attach one end of the line to the crossbar inside of the inner cradle. Run the line over the boat, making sure that it is laying straight across the boat--not snagged on a hatch or deck hardware. Grab the free end and pull it tight with one hand, marking a spot about a foot above the crossbar with the other hand. Tie a loop at that spot. Run the free end under the crossbar inside of the outer cradle then feed the free end through the loop. Pull tight and secure with a trucker's hitch. Check the lines periodically.

Use a security cable to discourage thieves and improve your peace of mind. Many boats are available with holes or permanently fixed metal cleats large enough to thread a cable through. If your boat doesn't have a place to attach the cable, wrap the cable tightly around the boat. In either case, lock the cable ends to your rack.

Most auto insurance policies will not cover your boat if it's stolen while on your car, so schedule theft coverage for your boat through your household insurance.

Figure 16   Trucker's Hitch

1. Make a loop and run the free end through.

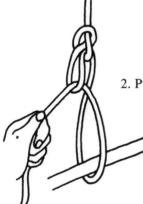

2. Pull on the free end to snug the line.

3. Secure with a half-hitch.

In the Air

Three quarters of our world's surface is covered with water—a heady thought when you're a paddler with an itch to travel. But distant destinations often mean flying and that's where the trouble begins—show up unprepared at check-in with a load of gear and a kayak and you're looking for trouble.

No major airline I've contacted has any specific policy regarding accepting kayaks as either checked baggage or freight. Most carriers will allow kayaks as freight on a space available basis. Unfortunately, air freight is very expensive and the cost of shipping a boat will often exceed the price of the paddler's ticket.

If you plan to fly often, consider an inflatable or breakdown boat. Most airlines will accept them without question as checked baggage and you'll eliminate the biggest problem encountered by traveling paddlers.

Pack your gear neatly. A jumble of gear bags with dangling straps increases your chances of losing equipment, infuriating baggage handlers and alienating check-in personnel. Every bag should be clearly marked, inside and out, with your name and destination. To protect your home while you're away, only the inside tag should have your home address.

APPENDIX I
GLOSSARY OF TERMS

Aft: Toward the stern from the cockpit.

Bailer: A scoop used to remove water from inside the kayak.

Beam: The widest part of the kayak.

Bearing: The direction to a landmark.

Blade: The flat part of a paddle.

Bow: The front end of the kayak.

Bulkhead: A waterproof wall dividing sections of the interior of the kayak.

Centerline: An imaginary line running lengthwise, dividing the kayak into equal left and right halves.

Coaming: The lip that surrounds the cockpit where the spray skirt attaches.

Cockpit: The opening in the kayak's deck where the paddler sits.

Course: The direction you want to go.

Deck: The top half of the kayak.

Dry Suit: A waterproof garment with watertight seals at the neck, wrists and ankles.

Face: The portion of the paddle blade designed to push against the water.

Feathered: Paddle blades rotated off the same eplane on the axis of the paddle shaft.

Forward: Toward the bow from the cockpit.

Gel-coat: The abrasion-resistant outer layer in a molded fiberglass/resin kayak.

Heading: The direction the kayak is pointed.

Hull: The bottom half of a kayak.

Life Vest: A foam-filled vest worn for flotation.

Line of Position: A range on which you are located.

Painters: Lines at the bow and stern of the kayak.

PFD: Personal Flotation Device. See life vest.

Range: A line on a chart extended from a straight road or shoreline, or from the alignment of two landmarks.

Shaft: The round tube connecting the paddle blades.

Spray skirt: Water-tight seal between the paddler and the kayak's coaming.

Stern: The back end of a kayak.

Trim: The bow to stern balance of the kayak.

Wetsuit: Garment that insulates by trapping water next to the skin beneath a layer of closed-cell neoprene foam.

APPENDIX II
SUGGESTED READING

Books

Bascom, Willard. *Waves and Beaches*. Anchor Books, 1980.

Burch, David. *Fundamentals of Kayak Navigation*. The Globe Pequot Press, 1987.

Daniel, Linda. *Kayak Cookery*, Globe Pequot Press, 1986.

Dowd, John. *Sea Kayaking: A Manual for Long Distance Touring*. University of Washington Press, 1988.

Forgey, William, MD. *Hypothermia: Death by Exposure*. ICS Books, 1985.

Hutchison, Derek. *Derek C. Hutchinson's Guide to Sea Kayaking*. The Globe Pequot Press, 1985.

Sutherland, Audrey. *Paddling Hawaii: An Insider's Guide to Exploring the Secluded Coves, Jungle Streams, and Wild Coasts of the Hawaiian Islands*. The Mountaineers, 1988.

Washburne, Randal. *Coastal Kayaker's Manual: A Complete Guide to Skills, Gear, and Sea Sense*. The Globe Pequot Press, 1989.

Periodicals

Sea Kayaker An information-packed resource. Published quarterly. 6327 Seaview Ave. N.W., Seattle, WA 98107

Canoe Covers a broad spectrum of paddling subjects including sea kayaking. Published six times a year, including an annual buyers' guide with complete listings of boats and accessories. P.O. Box 3146, Kirkland, WA 98083

APPENDIX III
EQUIPMENT CHECKLIST

Day Trip

Kayak
Paddle
Spare paddle
Life vest
Spray skirt
Buoyancy bags
Dry bags
Recovery gear
Whistle/air horn
Emergency signal kit
Weather radio
Binoculars
Pump
Sponge
Towline
Chart & case
Compass

Wrist-watch
Tide tables
Current chart
Rain wear
Wind shell
Pile jacket
Change of clothes
Pogies
Footwear
Sun hat
Sunglasses
Wet suit
Water bottle
Flashlight
Sunscreen
Insect repellant
Matches/lighter

Duct tape
Screwdriver
Small vice-grip pliers
Tarp
Line (100 feet parachute cord)
Towel
Emergency blanket
Basic first aid kit
Toilet paper
Trowel
Pee bottle

Overnight, add:
Tent
Sleeping bag
Sleeping pad
Cook kit
Utensils
Stove
Food
Fuel
Water bag
Hatchet or saw
Extra clothes
Repair kit
Toilet kit
Day pack
Spare sunglasses

APPENDIX IV
RESOURCES

Mail Order Suppliers

Recreational Equipment Incorporated (REI)
P.O. Box 88125
Seattle, Washington 98138

Pacific Water Sports
16205 Pacific Highway South
Seattle, Washington 98188

SEDA Products
P.O. Box 997
Chula Vista, California 92012

LL Bean. Inc.
Freeport, Maine 04033

Dealer Information

To find your nearest sea kayak retailer, contact the Trade Association of Sea Kayaking. They offer a free worldwide membership directory, listing retailers, manufacturers, and tour companies. TASK, P.O. Box 84144, Seattle, WA 98124

Charts

U.S.

National Ocean Services
Distribution Division (N/CG33)
Riverdale, MD 20737

Canada

Canadian Hydrographic Service
Department of Fisheries and Oceans
Institute of Ocean Sciences, Patricia Bay
9860 West Saanich Road, P.O. Box 6000
Sidney, B.C. V8L 4B2

Worldwide

Captain's Nautical Supply
1914 Fourth Ave.
Seattle, WA 98101

APPENDIX V
SYMPOSIA

May
Alaska Pacific University Kayak Symposium
APU Campus, Anchorage, Alaska
APU Student Activities
4101 University Drive
Anchorage, AK 99508

June
Mystic Sea Kayaking Symposium
Mystic, Connecticut
Mystic Valley Bikes
26 Williams Avenue
Mystic, CT 06355

Inland Sea Kayak Symposium
Bayfield, Wisconsin
Trek and Trail
P.O. Box 906
Bayfield, WI 54814

West Michigan Coastal Kayaking Symposium
North Muskegon, Michigan
Lumbertown Canoe and Kayak
1822 Oak Avenue
North Muskegon, MI 49445

August
Atlantic Coast Sea Kayaking Symposium
Castine, Maine
Public Clinic Program
L.L. Bean
Casco Street
Freeport, ME 04033

Great Lakes Kayak Touring Symposium
Grand Marais, Michigan
3721 Shallow Brook
Bloomfield Hills, MI 48013

September
West Coast Sea Kayaking Symposium
Port Townsend, Washington
Trade Association of Sea Kayaking
P.O. Box 84144
Seattle, WA 98124

INDEX

INDEX *(continued)*